The Three Little Kittens

www.englishhillbooks.studio

Copyright © Joan Gallup Grimord

First printing 2021

Edited by Erroll Imre

All rights reserved. No part of this book may be reproduced or transmitted in any form or by any means whatsoever without express permission from the author/illustrator.

This book belongs to:

....

Three little kittens, watch them play in the snow in their mittens.

They play in the snow,

making snowballs and fun.

Fun furry kittens wearing their mittens!

But three little kittens grow tired of play ...

and begin to think about home.

Mother stands at the door, waiting for kittens, for she has just baked a pie.

But the three little kittens ... oh no! They lost their mittens! And they began to cry, "Oh, mommy dear, we sadly fear, our mittens we have lost!"

"What? You've lost your mittens? You naughty kittens! Then you shall have no pie."

So the three little kittens, who lost their mittens, went out in the snow to spy, to look for their mittens in the drifts and hills, to look for their mittens, those naughty kittens.

They looked, and they looked in the snow.

The three little kittens, they found their mittens!
And they began to cry, "Oh, mommy dear! See here!
See here! Our mittens we have found!"

"What, found your mittens? You sweet little kittens! Then you shall have some pie! Purr, purr, yes, you shall have some pie!"

"But first, let's set out your mittens to dry!"

So they hung all the mittens to dry. All in a row, before the warm hearth, all in a row to dry.

The kittens sat ready with plates and spoons. Mother served each one and purred, "I'll check on your mittens while you eat pie. I will look to see if your mittens are dry!" And she left the room while the kittens ate pie!

But when Mother returned, what did she see?

Three messy kittens, with paw prints of pie on the floor and wall ... oh my!

"Oh, you messy kittens! What have you done to my kitchen? No bed for my kittens. You must clean up from pie!"

"Oh, mommy dear!" And they picked up their mittens, now dry, and wore their mittens to clean up pie!

They rubbed and they scrubbed with their mittens, and they cleaned up the kitchen.

"Look, mommy dear, we have cleaned up our pie!"

"But little kittens, my naughty kittens, look at the mess you've made of your mittens!" For the mittens were dirty from pie.

So into the tub, she put her kittens ... into the bath with pie and mittens. Now scrubby with bubbles, the kittens all clean; they cleaned their mittens, ready to dry.

"Oh, mother dear, we've cleaned our mittens. Our mittens are ready to dry!"

"Oh, you sweet little kittens, my sweet little kittens!" said mother, so happy as pie.

So they hung up their mittens to dry.

Mother put to bed her kittens, kissing each on the nose goodnight.

"God bless my sweet little kittens."

Good night!

Eliza Lee Cabot Follen initially penned *The Three Little Kittens* in the early 1800s; however, its roots may go back to old English folk rhymes centuries before. Many different versions of the poem have been published and illustrated in books for children over the years.

Joan always loved the poem from her childhood and was thrilled to do a retelling and illustrated rendition. Hers becomes a bedtime story about lively little kittens and a mother's reaction to them, including expressions of discipline, patience, reason, and love. She hopes you enjoy her adaptation, along with her illustrations, and that the book may become a favorite story for your family to read together.

English Hill Books

Book titles by Joan Gallup Grimord:

Silly Animal ABC's

Silly 123's

Let's go to the Fair

Cinderella Hippo

Hippo and Gretel

Where is God

Goldilocks and the Three Bears

www.englishhillbooks.studio

Made in the USA
Columbia, SC
18 September 2021